Valentino

B
B

God

can handle it...

for Mothers

God
can handle it...
for Mothers

Compiled and Edited by Carlene Ward

BRIGHTON BOOKS
Nashville, TN 37205

ISBN 1-887655-89-1

The ideas expressed in this book (but not Bible Verses) are not, in all cases, exact quotations, as some have been edited for clarity and brevity. In all cases, the author has attempted to maintain the speaker's original intent. In some cases, material for this book was obtained from secondary sources, primarily print media. While every effort was made to ensure the accuracy of these sources, the accuracy cannot be guaranteed. For additions, deletions, corrections or clarifications in future editions of this text, please write BRIGHTON BOOKS.

Printed in the United States of America
Layout by Sue Gerdes
1 2 3 4 5 6 7 8 9 10 • 98 99 00 01 02 03 04 05

For my mother, Terry,

my best friend

Table of Contents

A Message to Readers

God chooses to work through people. Many have touched my life and made it better, but I am particularly indebted to a special group of "moms." These women, all members of Bible study groups, were always ready to share their insights on the challenges and rewards of motherhood. They have also shared their strength, hope, courage, love and friendship.

Mother Teresa once said, "In order to keep a lamp burning, you have to keep putting oil in it." In the company of these mothers, I have found the oil for my own lamp. I pray that the message of this book will add oil to *your* lamp and that His word will be a light to your path.

Carlene,
Mother of Mollie and Dan

1

Motherhood

"Motherhood," states Erma Bombeck, "is the second oldest profession." Thus it would seem that the mother's how-to manual would be complete by now. But all mothers are different and require different solutions to the inevitable challenges of caring for a family.

Despite their differences, mothers everywhere share a common bond; they have all carried within themselves a creation of God. All mothers have worked hand-in-hand with the Creator to bring new life into the world.

The next time you find yourself feeling "down" or unappreciated, remember that as a mother you are in partnership with God. You have gifted this world with a child: a unique life of unlimited potential. You and God are hard at work to make the world a better place — and, as a mother, yours is one of the most important jobs this side of heaven.

Of all the rights
of women,
the greatest is
to be a mother.

Lin Yu-t'ang

A good woman is the best thing on earth.... The church owes a debt to our faithful women which we can never estimate, to say nothing of the debt we owe in our homes to godly wives and mothers.

Vance Havner

...then choose for yourselves this day whom you will serve...But as for me and my household, we will serve the Lord.
Joshua 24:15 NIV

I'd gone through life believing in
the strength and competencies of others;
never in my own. Now, dazzled, I discovered
that my capacities were real. It was like finding
a fortune in the lining of an old coat.

Joan Mills

A sobering thought: What if, right at this
very moment, I were living up to
my full potential?

Jane Wagner

*...and he asked them, "Do you believe that I am
able to do this? According to your faith
will it be done for you."
Matthew 9:28-29 NIV*

I love people. I love my family, my
children...but inside myself is a place where
I live all alone, and that's where I renew
those springs that never dry up.

Pearl Buck

If you let decisions be made for you,
you'll be trampled.

Betsy White

Being a mother is rewarding to one's female
instincts, trying to one's nerves, physically
exhausting, emotionally both frustrating
and satisfying, and, above all, not to be
undertaken lightly.

Dr. Margaret Raphael

*Listen to advice and accept instruction,
and in the end you will be wise.
Proverbs 19:20 NIV*

A woman is the full circle.
    Within her is the power to create,
      to nurture, and to transform.

Diane Mariechild

The mother is the most precious possession
    of the nation, so precious that society
    advances its highest well-being when
    it protects the functions of the mother.

Ellen Key

*However, as it is written: "No eye has seen,
no ear has heard, no mind has conceived what
God has prepared for those who love him."
1 Corinthians 2:9 NIV*

All that I am or hope to
be I owe to my mother.

Abraham Lincoln

As a mother, my job is to take care of the possible and trust God with the impossible.

Ruth Bell Graham

The Lord is my strength and song;
He has become my salvation.
Exodus 15:2 NIV

A mother is a person who
needs to remember she is a person.

Mary Eleanore Rich

I guess what I've really discovered is
the humanizing effect of children in my life,
stretching me, humbling me. Maybe my thighs
aren't as thin as they used to be, maybe my
getaways aren't as glamorous. Still I like the
woman that motherhood has
helped me to become.

Susan Lapinski

There are times when the needs of the
care-giver are more important than the needs
of the child. We must consider the care-givers
need for refueling — for care, nurturance,
support — to counteract the insidious myth
that mothers are an endless source of love and
emotional sustenance.

Jane Swigart

Motherhood brings us much joy as ever,
but it still brings boredom, exhaustion, and
sorrow too. Nothing else ever will make you
as happy or as sad, as proud or as tired, for
nothing is quite as hard as helping a person
develop his or her own individuality,
especially while you struggle
to keep your own.

Marguerite Kelly/Elia Parsons

Being a mother, as far as I can tell, is
a constantly evolving process of adapting to
the needs of your child while also changing
and growing as a person in your own right.

Deborah Insel

*You can be sure the Lord will
protect you from harm.
Proverbs 3:26 CEV*

A mother understands what her child doesn't say.

Yiddish Proverb

Speak, Lord: for thy servant heareth.
1 Samuel 3:9

Mother is the name for God on the lips and in the hearts of little children.

William Makepeace Thackeray

Her children arise up, and call her blessed.
Proverbs 31:28

2

Moving Mountains
And Kids

An old saying reminds us that "People who want to move mountains must start by carrying away small stones." For many mothers, it seems *easier* to move mountains than to move those sleepy kids out of their beds each morning. Such are the challenges of motherhood.

Whether you are moving mountains, kids, or both, remember that it takes patience and a steady hand, so don't give up. Just do your best and keep carrying away small stones...or small people! And leave the rest up to God.

Lord, please give me patience...but give it to me fast.

Anonymous

...the moment we get tired in the waiting, God's Spirit is right alongside helping us along.
Romans 8:26 The Message

We need to be patient with our children
in the same way God is patient with us.

Renee Jordan

A mother's patience is like a tube of
toothpaste: It's never quite gone.

Unknown

*I waited patiently for the Lord; he turned to me
and heard my cry...He put a new
song in my mouth....*
Psalm 40:1,3 NIV

All the flowers of all the tomorrows are
in the seeds of today.

Anne Outland

The willingness to accept responsibility
for one's own life is the source
from which self-respect springs.

Joan Didion

We've come a distance,
but we still have a distance to go.

Traditional Saying

*But you must learn to endure everything,
so that you will be completely mature and not
lacking in anything.
James 1:3 CEV*

Be not afraid of growing slowly; be afraid only of standing still.

Chinese Proverb

We do not want you to become lazy, but to initiate those who through faith and patience inherit what has been promised.
Hebrews 6:12 NIV

P atience achieves more than force.

Edmund Burke

G od often permits us to be perplexed
so that we may learn patience.

T. J. Bach

P eace within makes beauty without.

English Proverb

In your patience possess ye your souls.
Luke 21:19

Love is patient, love is kind...

1 Corinthians 13:4 NIV

What cannot be removed becomes
lighter through patience.

Quintus Horatius

Perhaps there is only one cardinal sin:
impatience. Because of impatience we were
driven out of paradise; because of impatience
we cannot return.

Franz Kafla

The way I see it, if you want the rainbow,
you've got to put up with the rain.

Dolly Parton

The toddler is the world's most
hard-nosed opponent of law and order.

James Dobson

Behold, we count them happy which endure.
James 5:11

Children are like clocks... they must be allowed to run.

James Dobson

A man's wisdom gives him patience...
Proverbs 19:11 NIV

Patience is the companion of wisdom.
St. Augustine

We can do anything we want to do if
we stick to it long enough.
Helen Keller

The strongest of all warriors are
these two: time and patience.
Leo Tolstoy

*God is my strength and my power; and
he maketh my way perfect.
2 Samuel 22:33*

Teach us, O Lord, the disciplines of patience, for to wait is often harder than to work.

Peter Marshall

Remembering without ceasing your work of faith, and labor of love, and patience of hope in our Lord Jesus Christ...
1 Thessalonians 1:3

Patient waiting is often the highest way of doing God's will.

Saint Francis of Sales

...be patient with everyone.
1 Thessalonians 5:14 NIV

3

Teach Your Children Well

Stephen Covey once observed, "If we do not teach our children, society will. And they — and we — will live with the results." These words are frightful but true. Mothers, therefore, must strive to teach their children well...and keep on teaching them throughout life.

On the pages that follow, we consider the value of a mother's knowledge and experience. Children — of all ages — should still remember that mother knows best. In life, school is always in session, and mom, as we all know, is almost always the best teacher!

Most mothers are instinctive philosophers.
Harriet Beecher Stowe

Our children do not follow our words
but our actions.
James Baldwin

The hearing and the training of a child
is a woman's wisdom.
Alfred Lord Tennyson

*Teach them the decrees and laws, and show
them the way to live and the duties
they are to perform.
Exodus 18:20 NIV*

Be careful with truth
towards children; to a
child, the parent or
teacher is the
representative
of justice.

Margaret Fuller

*And thou shalt teach them ordinances and laws,
and shall show them the way wherein they must
walk, and the work that they must do.
Exodus 18:20*

There is so much to teach, and the time goes so fast.

Erma Bombeck

So teach us to number our days, that we may apply our hearts unto wisdom.
Psalm 90:12

No living person can live well
without reading and time for reflection.
Alexandra Stoddard

The teacher, if indeed wise, does not
bid you to enter the house of wisdom, but
leads you to the threshold
of your own mind.
Khalil Gibran

What greater work is there than training
the mind and forming the habits
of the young?
St. John of Chrysostom

*In everything set them an example
by doing what is good...
Titus 2:7 NIV*

Education is useless
without the Bible.

Noah Webster

Faith is greater than learning.

Martin Luther

Education without religion, as useful as it is,
seems rather to make a man
a more clever devil.

C. S. Lewis

A little learning is a dangerous thing.

Alexander Pope

*The book of the law... you will meditate day and
night that you may observe to do all that is
written therein, for then you shall make your
way prosperous and you shall
have good success.
Joshua 1:8*

...d doesn't mean giving in
...hims; to love him is to bring
...best in him, to teach him
to love what is difficult.

Nadia Boulanger

Your children learn more of your faith during
the bad times than they do during
the good times.

Beverly LaHaye

The school will teach children how to read,
but the environment of the home must
teach them what to read. The school
can teach them how to think,
but the home must teach
them what to believe.

Charles A. Wells

It is desirable that children be kind,
appreciative and pleasant. Those qualities
should be taught and not hoped for.

James Dobson

Train up a child in the way he should go: and when he is old, he will not depart from it.

Proverbs 22:6

In the effort to give good and comforting
answers to the young questioners whom
we love, we very often arrive at good and
comforting answers ourselves.

Ruth Goode

If you want to be listened to,
you should put in time listening.

Marge Piercy

The walks and talks we have with
our 2-year-olds in red boots have
a great deal to do with the values
they will cherish as adults.

Edith Hunter

He who walks with the wise grows wise...
Proverbs 13:20 NIV

There is no influence so powerful as that of a mother.

Sarah J. Hale

Give me understanding, and I will keep your law and obey it with all my heart.
Psalm 119:34 NIV

There are tones of voice that mean more than words.

Robert Frost

*And they heard the voice of the Lord God
walking in the garden in the cool of the day...
Genesis 3:8*

4

Steady as She Goes

Your daily to-do list seems to have everyone's name on it. The morning drive to school dissolves into evening bedside prayers. And another amazing day in the life of a mother is done.

One mother described her life as a tangled ball of yarn with many ends hanging out. She spoke for mothers everywhere when she explained that she didn't know which end of the yarn to pick first. The solution to her dilemma was found when she was able to restore a sense of balance in her life.

So take time for yourself — quiet time. Be flexible ; maintain your sense of balance. And while you're at it, why not let God help organize that to-do list? What may be hard for you is easy for Him.

It's not so much how busy you are, but why you are so busy. The bee is praised; the mosquito is swatted.

Marie O'Conner

We need time to dream, time to remember, and time to reach the infinite. Time to be.

Gladys Taber

...seek peace, and pursue it.
Psalm 34:14 NIV

When your schedule leaves you drained
and stressed to exhaustion, it's time to
give up something. Delegate. Say no.
It's like cleaning out a closet: After
a while it gets easier to get rid of things.
You discover that you really didn't
need them anyway.

Marilyn Ruman

Time is the stuff of which life is made.

Benjamin Franklin

The quieter you become,
the more you can hear.

Baba Ram Dass

*Come unto me, all ye that labour and are heavy
laden, and I will give you rest.*
Matthew 11:28

Peace is seeing a sunset and knowing whom to thank.

Unknown

...we are being renewed day by day.
2 Corinthians 4:16 NIV

You must learn to be still in the midst of activity and to be vibrantly alive in repose.

Indira Gandhi

Steep your life in God-reality, God-initiative, God-provisions. Don't worry about missing out. You'll find your everyday human concerns will be met.
Matthew 6:33 The Message

Finish every day and be done with it. You have done what you could. Some blunders and absurdities no doubt crept in; forget them as soon as you can. Tomorrow is a new day. Begin it well.

Ralph Waldo Emerson

...weeping may remain for a night, but rejoicing comes in the morning. Psalm 30:5

Concentrate on the issues that are most
important to you and minimize or ignore
the non-essentials.

James C. Numan

Insanity is doing the same thing over
and over again but expecting
different results.

Rita Mae Brown

It takes all the running we can do
just to keep in the same place.

Lewis Carroll

Don't hurry, don't worry. You're only here
for a short time. So be sure to stop
and smell the roses.

Walter Hagen

The ant is knowing and wise; but he doesn't know enough to take a vacation.

Clarence Day

*...forsake the foolish, and live;
and go in the way of understanding.*
Proverbs 9:6

Half our life is spent trying to find
    something to do with the time we have
       rushed through life trying to save.

Will Rogers

There is more to life than
             increasing its speed.

Gandhi

There's nothing quite so valuable as work.
  That's why it is a good idea to leave some
       for tomorrow.

Marian Dolliver

Six days thou shalt work,
but on the seventh day
thou shall rest.

Exodus 34:21

Take rest; a field that has rested gives a bountiful crop.

Ovid

Rest in the Lord, and wait patiently for him.
Psalm 37:7

Things which matter most must never be at
the mercy of things which matter least.

Goethe

Part of the frustration of the hurried life is
that it has a way of trivializing
our commitments.

Tim Kimmel

Burned-out kids often have
burned-out parents.

Anonymous

Be still and know that I am God.
Psalm 46:10

We move through life in such a distracted way that we do not even take the time to wonder if any of the things we think, say, or do are worth thinking, saying, or doing.

Henri Nouwen

The darn trouble with cleaning the house is it gets dirty the next day anyway; so skip a week if you have to. The children are the most important thing.

Barbara Bush

Too much love never spoils children. Children become spoiled when we substitute "presents" for "presence."

Dr. Anthony P. Witham

Lo, children are a heritage of the Lord ...
Psalm 127:3

No one ever gives us time. And we never find time. We must seize time.

Alexandra Stoddard

He hath made everything beautiful in his time.
Ecclesiastes 3:11

Life, at best, becomes a divine balancing act
in order to create wisdom and harmony.

Alexandra Stoddard

I must govern the clock,
not be governed by it.

Golda Meir

Balance — the key to peace and wisdom.

Azura

There is nothing more terrible than activity without insight.

Thomas Carlyle

But seek first his kingdom and his righteousness, and all these things will be given to you as well.
Matthew 6:33 NIV

Every morning is a gift.
I've learned how precious
each moment is.

Ben Short

I will sing aloud of thy mercy in the morning.
Psalm 59:16

5

We Are Family

The need to belong is basic in every person. That's why families are so important: We belong to our families and our families belong to us.

God says you are His and no one can pluck you from His hand. There is great comfort in this fact. On the pages that follow we examine the importance of family...your family and God's.

What we learn within the family are the most unforgettable lessons that our lives will ever teach us.

Maggie Scarf

And that these days should be remembered and kept throughout every generation, every family.
Esther 9:28

Children find comfort
in flaws, ignorance
and insecurities similar
to their own. I love my
mother for letting me
see hers.

Erma Bombeck

*...for all have sinned and fallen short of
the glory of God.
Romans 3:23 NIV*

Children are the anchors that
hold a mother to life.

Sophocles

One of the oldest human needs is having
someone to wonder where you are when
you don't come home at night.

Margaret Mead

There are all those early memories;
one cannot get another set;
one has only these.

Willa Cather

Bringing up a family
should be an adventure,
not an anxious discipline
in which everybody is
constantly graded
for performance.

Milton R. Saperstein

*He that troubleth his own house shall
inherit the wind.
Proverbs 11:29*

It takes a hundred men
to make an encampment
but one woman
to make a home.

Robert G. Ingersoll

There are innumerable people who have
a wide choice between saving money
and giving their children the best possible
opportunities. The decision is usually
in favor of the children.

Eleanor Roosevelt

To nourish children and raise them against
odds is in any time, any place, more valuable
then to fix bolts in cars or
design nuclear weapons.

Marilyn French

The best use of life is to spend it
for something that outlasts life.

William James

*... My family and I are going to worship and
serve the Lord.
Joshua 24:15 CEV*

The way you treat any relationship in the
family will eventually affect every relationship
in the family.

Stephen Covey

If one examines the secret behind a
championship football team, a magnificent
orchestra, or a successful business,
the principal ingredient is
invariably discipline.

James Dobson

*He opens their ear to discipline and commands
that they turn from iniquity.
Job 36:10*

Make sure that you
never forget the Lord
or disobey his laws
and teachings.

Deuteronomy 8:11 CEV

Love is blind...
but marriage
restores its sight.

Georg Christoph Lichtenberg

*Open my eyes that I may behold
wonderous things ....
Psalm 119:18*

A successful marriage is not a gift,
it is an achievement.

Ann Landers

A successful marriage is always a triangle:
a man, a woman and God.

Cecil Myers

Success in marriage is more than finding the
right person; it is being the right person.

Robert Browning

No kingdom divided can
stand — neither can
a household.

Christine de Pisan

Whatever the times, one thing will never
change: Fathers and mothers, if you have
children, they must come first. Your success
as a family, our success as a society, depends
not on what happens in the White House,
but what happens inside your house.

Barbara Bush

Healthy families are our
greatest national resource.

Dolores Curran

As the family goes, so goes the nation and
so goes the whole world in which we live.

Pope John Paul II

*...and the mother of the child said, "As the Lord
lives and as thy soul lives
I will not leave thee."
2 Kings 4:30*

Family life! The United Nations is child's play compared to the tugs and splits and need to understand and forgive in any family.

May Sarton

*These commandments that I give you today
are to be upon your hearts.
Impress them on your children…
Deuteronomy 6:6, 7 NIV*

6

Dream a Little Dream

Someone once said, "Only those who can see the invisible can do the impossible." Our dreams are fueled by the heartbeat of our passions and nurtured by the support of our fellow dreamers. Our dreams keep us alive; we must never stop dreaming, and we must never stop encouraging others to do likewise.

It has been written, "Develop your dreams and you create passion...Develop the dreams of others and you create heaven." Mothers play an important role by teaching their children to dream and then to go about living their dreams. Here's how …

The future belongs to those who believe in the beauty of their dreams.

Eleanor Roosevelt

…Forgetting what is behind and straining toward what is ahead, I press on toward the goal to win the prize for which God has called me heavenward in Christ Jesus.
Philippians 3:13,14 NIV

Nothing happens unless first a dream.

Carl Sandburg

I will lift up mine eyes unto the hills,
from whence cometh my help.
Psalm 121:1

Too many people put
their dreams "on hold."
It takes an uncommon
amount of guts to put
your dreams on the line,
to hold them up and say,
"How good or bad am I?"
That's where the courage
comes in.

Erma Bombeck

*Wait on the Lord; be of good courage and he
shall strengthen thine heart.
Psalm 27:14*

When we listen to dreams, we change;
and when dreams are heard, they change us.

Fraser Boa

Your own words are the bricks and mortar of
the dreams you want to realize.

Sonia Choquette

It is never too late to dream or start
something new.

Luci Swindoll

You see things and you say, "Why?"
I dream things that never were and say,
"Why not?"

George Bernard Shaw

To dare is to lose one's footing momentarily.
Not to dare is to lose oneself completely.

Kierkegaard

If one advances confidently in the
direction of his dreams and endeavors
to love the life which he has imagined,
he will meet with a success unexpected
in common hours.

Henry David Thoreau

Faith can put a candle in the darkest night.

Margaret Sangster

For with God nothing
shall be impossible.

Luke 1:37

If one is lucky, a
solitary fantasy
can totally transform
one million realities.

Maya Angelou

S addle up your dreams before
you ride them.

Mary Webb

E ven if you are on the right track,
you will get run over if you just sit there.

Will Rogers

L ive out your imagination, not your history.

Stephen Covey

I was not looking for my dreams to interpret
my life but rather for my life to interpret
my dreams.

Susan Sontag

...Run in such a way as to get the prize.
I Corinthians 9:24 NIV

The word which God has written on
    the brow of every man is *hope*.

Victor Hugo

Sad soul, take comfort, nor forget,
    The sunrise never failed us yet.

Celia Thaxter

Tis always morning somewhere.

Henry Wadsworth Longfellow

*My voice shalt thou hear in the morning O Lord;
in the morning will I direct my prayer unto thee,
and will look up.*
Psalm 5:3

It's a funny thing about life; if you refuse
to accept anything but the best,
you very often get it.

Somerset Maugham

If you don't daydream and plan
things out in your imagination, you never get
there. So you have to start someplace.

Robert Duvall

Hope in the Lord but exert yourself.

Russian Proverb

What time I am afraid, I will trust in thee.
Psalm 56:3

God's gifts put man's best dreams to shame.

Elizabeth Barrett Browning

The Lord is my shepherd; I shall not want.
Psalm 23:1

Seize this very minute. What you dream to do, you must begin.

Goethe

For you have been my hope, O Sovereign Lord,
my confidence since my youth.
Psalm 71:5

Second to the right and
straight on 'til morning.

J.M. Barrie from Peter Pan

*For ye shall go out with joy and
be led forth with peace....
Isaiah 55:12*

7

Batten Down the Hatches

A favorite quote from Louisa May Alcott reads, "I'm not afraid of storms for I am learning to sail my ship." The ship of motherhood must, from time to time, sail on stormy seas. But even when the storm clouds loom very dark on the horizon, mothers keep sailing — and learning.

Day after day, smooth seas or choppy, mothers make decisions great and small. The responsibility of raising children takes courage, patience and faith. So all hands on deck; batten down the hatches; full steam ahead; and one more thing: Let God steer the ship. With Him at the helm, there's nothing to fear.

You must do the thing you think you cannot do.

Eleanor Roosevelt

Be strong and courageous...for the Lord your God goes with you; he will never leave you or forsake you.
Deuteronomy 3:6 NIV

A contempt that drives you through
fires and makes you risk everything
will make you better than you ever knew
you could be.

Willa Cather

The best way out is through.

Robert Frost

This is courage: to bear unflinchingly
what heaven sends.

Euripides

*...don't be afraid...those who are with us are
more than those who are with them.*
2 Kings 6:16

Trust in yourself. Your perceptions are
often far more accurate than you
are willing to believe.

Claudia Black

You've got to play the hand that's dealt you.
There may be pain in that hand,
but you play it.

James Brady

*And he said unto me, My grace is sufficient for
thee: for my strength is made perfect
in weakness.*
2 Corinthians 12:9

You cannot discover new oceans,
  unless you have the courage to lose
    sight of the shore.

Unknown

Life shrinks or expands in proportion
    to one's courage.

Anaïs Nin

To get where you want to go, you must
    keep on keeping on.

Norman Vincent Peale

Be of good courage and do it.
Ezra 10:4b

The real voyage of discovery consists not in seeking new landscapes but in having new eyes.

Marcel Proust

*Open my eyes so I can see what you show me
of your miracle-wonders.
Psalm 119:18 The Message*

We are all pencils in the hand of God.

Mother Teresa

*God rewrote the text of my life when I opened
the book of my heart to his eyes.
Psalm 18:24 The Message*

Courage is the price that
life exacts for granting
peace. The soul that
knows it not knows
no release from
little things....

Amelia Earhart

Yea, though I walk
through the valley of the
shadow of death, I will
fear no evil: for thou art
with me....

Psalm 23:4

It takes great courage to faithfully follow
what we know to be true.

Sara Anderson

The mothers of brave men must
themselves be brave.

Mary Bell Washington

Great successes never come without risks.

Flavious Josephus

In any moment of decision, the best thing
you do is the right thing; the next best thing
is the wrong thing, and the worst
thing you can do is nothing.

Theodore Roosevelt

*I can do all things through Christ
which strengthens me.
Philippians 4:13 NIV*

8

The Joys of Motherhood

The joy of giving life is beyond words — but all mothers know the feeling. The pain of childbirth quickly gives way to an unmatched surge of exultation. And that's only the beginning. The joys of raising children are simply too numerous to count (and that's good because most mothers are far too busy *to keep count*).

God intends for all of us to live abundant, joy-filled lives. And when we put God in charge of our lives, the joy takes care of itself.

All mothers are rich when they love their children. There are no poor mothers, no ugly ones, no old ones. Their love is always the most beautiful of joys.

Maurice Maeterlinck

...being content is as good as an endless feast.
Proverbs 15:15

When you look at your life, the greatest happiness is family happiness.

Dr. Joyce Brothers

A merry heart doeth good like medicine....
Proverbs 17:22

All who would win joy must share it;
    happiness was born a twin.

Lord Byron

What we loosely call happiness is more
    a disposition than an attainment.

Sydney Harris

To love what you do and to feel
    that it matters — how could anything
      be more fun?

Katharine Graham

Today, I live in the quiet joyous
    expectation of good.

Ernest Holmes

But let all that put their trust in thee rejoice.

Psalm 5:11

Happiness is not a goal. It is a by-product.

Eleanor Roosevelt

Commit to the Lord whatever you do, and your plans will succeed.
Proverbs 16:3 NIV

What sunshine is to flowers, smiles are
to humanity. They are but trifles scattered
along life's pathway, but the good
they do is inconceivable.

Joseph Addison

TA-RA-RA-BOOM-DE-AY!!!

Henry J. Sayers

A frowning face repels. A smile reaches out
and attracts. Don't fence it in...
loosen up...smile!

Charles Swindoll

A happy heart makes the face cheerful....
Proverbs 15:13

Always laugh when you can;
      it is cheap medicine.

Lord Byron

He who laughs, lasts.

Anonymous

When my kids become wild and unruly,
      I use a nice, safe playpen.
      When they're finished,
      I climb out.

Erma Bombeck

The quickest way for a parent to get
      a child's attention is to sit down
      and look comfortable.

Lane Olinhouse

Be glad in the Lord.
Psalm 32:11

Of course I'd like to be the ideal mother. But I'm too busy raising children.

Family Circus Comic Strip

By Bill Keane

A good woman…[is]skilled in the crafts of home and hearth, diligent in homemaking. Proverbs 31:10,15 The Message

Train your child in the way in which you know you should have gone yourself.

C.H. Spurgeon

*I will instruct thee and teach thee in the way
which thou shalt go; I will guide thee
with mine eyes.*
Psalm 32:8

It goes without saying
that you should never
have more children than
you have car windows.

Erma Bombeck

We could never learn to be
   brave and patient if there were only
      joy in the world.

Helen Keller

The happiest people are those
   who do the most for others.

Booker T. Washington

Joy is not in things; it is in us.

Benjamin Franklin

*I bring you good news of great joy...Today in
the town of David a Savior has been born to
you; he is Christ the Lord.*
Luke 2:10,11 NIV

9

Friends Are Forever

What a privilege and comfort to have friends. Real friendship means not having to make explanations. Our friends understand us and accept us unconditionally — in good times and bad,

The encouragement of friends is one way that God supports us during the tough times. And in the good times, when we wish to share our joys, our friends double the pleasure.

You may be the independent sort and seemingly self-sufficient, but you still need meaningful friendships, especially if you're a busy mother. So take time — *or make time* — for friends. And while you're at it, take time for the friendly advice that follows.

Women best understand each others' language.

Teresa of Avila

I learned that to have a good friend is
the purest of all God's gifts, for it is
a love that has no exchange of payment.

Frances Farmer

Friendship — any close friendship — is
so various, made up of so many strands:
companionship, the sharing of laughter,
common work and common tastes.

Iris Origo

*A man that hath friends must show
himself friendly....
Proverbs 18:24*

You are justified in avoiding people who send you from their presence with less hope and strength to cope with life's problems than when you met them.

Ella Wheeler Wilcox

*Blessed is the man who does not walk
in the counsel of the wicked...
Psalm 1:1 NIV*

Wherever you are, it is your friends
who make your world.

William James

Friendship with oneself is all-important,
because without it one cannot be friends
with anyone else in the world.

Eleanor Roosevelt

It is one of the most beautiful compensations
of this life that no man can sincerely try
to help another without helping himself.

Ralph Waldo Emerson

*And let us consider how we may spur one
another on toward love and good deeds.
Hebrews 10:24 NIV*

Good company on a journey makes the way seem shorter.

Izaac Walter

*…there is a friend who sticks closer
than a brother.
Proverbs 18:24 NIV*

So long as we love, we serve. So long as
   we are loved by others, I would almost say
we are indispensable; and no man is useless
            while he has a friend.

Robert Louis Stevenson

A parent acquires all rights of
         the most sacred friendship.

Mary Wollstonecraft.

If you have made friends…there is always
   another chance for you…you may have a
      fresh start any moment you choose,
      for this thing we call failure is not
   the falling down, but the staying down.

Mary Pickford

A friend loves at all times….
Proverbs 17:17 NIV

Relationships with other people
have made my life incredibly rich.

Barbara Bush

Traveling in the company of those we love
is home in motion.

Leigh Hunt

Treat your friends as you do your picture,
and place them in their best light.

Jennie Jerome Churchill

...and every man is a friend to him
that giveth gifts.
Proverbs 19:6

We are here to help one another along life's journey.

William Bennett

Perhaps I will stay with you awhile…so that you can help me on my journey, wherever I go.
I Corinthians 16:6 NIV

It is my friends who have made the story
of my life.

Helen Keller

I always felt that the great high privilege,
relief and comfort of friendship was that
one had to explain nothing.

Katherine Mansfield

Trouble shared is trouble halved.

Dorothy Sayers

A good deed is never lost; he who sows
courtesy reaps friendship, and he who
plants kindness gathers love.

St. Basil

You have filled my heart with greater joy…
Psalm 4:7 NIV

It is the friends you can call up a 4:00 A.M. that matter.

Marlene Dietrich

*Which of you shall have a friend, and shall go
into him at midnight, and say unto him,
Friend, loan me three loaves?…
Luke 11:5*

The only way to have a friend is to be one.

Ralph Waldo Emerson

...for whatsoever a man soweth, that shall he also reap... And let us not be weary in well doing; for in due season we shall reap, if we faint not.
Galatians 6:7,9

<u>10</u>

LOVE

"…and the greatest of these is love."

Mother's love grows by giving.

Charles Lamb

Love is a great beautifier.

Louisa May Alcott

Love is a multiplication.

Marjory Stoneman Douglas

I do not love him because he is good.
I love him because he is my child.

Rabindraneth Tagore

For God so loved the
world that he gave his
only begotten Son, that
whosoever believeth
in him should not
perish, but have
everlasting life.

John 3:16

C hildren need love, especially
when they don't deserve it.

Harold Hulbert

W hat tigress is there that does not purr
over her young ones and
fawn upon them in tenderness?

St. Augustine

T o love is to receive a glimpse of heaven.

Karen Sunde

*Be ye therefore merciful, as your Father
also is merciful.
Luke 6:36*

There is no friendship, no love, like that of the mother for the child.

Henry Ward Beecher

*...learn first of all to put [your]
religion into practice by caring for [your]
own family...for this is pleasing to God.
1 Timothy 5:4 NIV*

Love

I looked on child rearing not only as
work and duty but as a profession that was
fully as interesting and challenging as any
honorable profession in the world and
one that demanded the best
that I could bring to it.

Rose Kennedy

No language can express the power and
beauty and heroism of a mother's love.

Edwin Chapin

Mother love is the fuel that enables
a normal human being to do the impossible.

Marion Garetty

Before you were conceived, I wanted you.
Before you were born, I loved you.
Before you were here and home,
I would die for you.
This is the miracle of love.

Maureen Hawkins

A mother's love perceives
no impossibilities.

Paddock

The things which are impossible with men are possible with God.

Luke 18:27

Love is a fruit in season and within reach of every hand.

Mother Teresa

...for God is love.
1 John 4:8

Love is the subtlest force in the world.

Gandhi

Forgiveness is the final form of love.

Reinhold Neibuhr

The first duty of love is to listen.

Paul Tillich

A mother's love! O Holy, boundless thing!
Fountain whose waters never cease to spring.

Marguerite Blessington

...with a mighty hand and outstretched arm; His
love endures forever.
Psalm 136:12 NIV

A mother's arms are made of tenderness
and children sleep in them.

Victor Hugo

I grew up knowing I was accepted and loved,
and that made an incredible difference.

Bernie Siegel

Never fear spoiling children by making
them happy. Happiness is the atmosphere
in which all good affections grow.

Ann Eliza Bray

Loving your children isn't enough if
you don't enjoy their company.

John Bradshaw

*... put [your] hope in God, who richly provides
us with everything for our enjoyment.
1 Timothy 6:17 NIV*

Life is the flower of which love is the honey.

Victor Hugo

*All things work together for good to them
that love God.
Romans 8:28*

I have decided to stick with love.
Hate is too great a burden to bear.

Martin Luther King, Jr.

Love is an act of endless forgiveness,
a tender look which becomes a habit.

Peter Ustinov

The ultimate lesson all of us have to learn
is unconditional love, which includes
not only others but ourselves as well.

Elisabeth Kübler-Ross

...let us love one another....
1 John 4:7 NIV

A mother's love is like a circle; it has
no beginning and no ending. It keeps
going around and around, always
expanding, touching everyone who
comes in contact with it.

Art Urban

Maternal love: a miraculous substance
which God multiplies as he divides it.

Victor Hugo

You don't have to deserve your mother's love.

Robert Frost

*May the Lord direct your hearts into God's love
and Christ's perseverance.
2 Thessalonians 3:5 NIV*

When Mother Teresa received her Nobel Prize, she was asked, "What can we do to promote world peace?" She replied, "Go home and love your family."

Let love and faithfulness never leave you; bind them around your neck, write them on the tablet of your heart.
Proverbs 3:3 NIV

When the evening of this life comes, we shall be judged on love.

St. John of the Cross

In the presence of love, miracles happen.

Robert Schuller

However, as it is written:
"No eye has seen, no ear
has heard, no mind has
conceived what God has
prepared for those
who love him."

1 Corinthians 2:9 NIV

And now these three
remain: faith, hope
and love. But the
greatest of
these is
love.

I Corinthians 13:13 NIV

Index of Quoted Sources

Sources

About the Author

Carlene Ward lives, writes and works in Nashville, Tennessee. She is a sought-after public speaker and the mother of two children, Mollie and Dan.

Carlene juggles career and family while attending First Baptist Church of Nashville where she is an active member.

About the
God Can Handle It
Series

God Can Handle It...for Mothers is part of a series by Brighton Books. Each title features inspirational quotations and relevant scripture passages. For more information, please call toll free: 1-800-256-8584.